This material supplements the *Cash Rules for Entrepreneurs* audio course. Visit **www.CashRulesforEntrepreneurs.com** to view the course and download additional materials, including a podcast and illustrations of the concepts.

I0485008

$CashRules for $Entrepreneurs

by Troy Schrock
Advisor Catalyst, Inc.

Cash Rules for Entrepreneurs is created with the permission of Bill McGuinness, whose book, *Cash Rules*, forms the foundation for much of the material presented here.

ActionCFO™ is a proven process created by Advisor Catalyst, Inc. It is specifically designed for use by certified CFO advisors who provide part-time CFO services to owners or CEOs of businesses with revenue between $2M and $20M. ActionCFO advisors customize the proprietary Financial Visibility and Control System™ to each client's needs.

For more information about how ActionCFO™ can help your organization, please visit **www.actioncfo.com**.

Contents

Introduction

On June 14, 2009 at Michigan International Speedway, NASCAR driver Mark Martin entered the final two laps of the race in third place, having never led at any point. Superstar driver Jimmie Johnson was in the lead, and Greg Biffle was close behind in second. Suddenly, Johnson ran out of gas, and Biffle seemed to be in line for the win. But then, with one lap to go, Biffle's car began sputtering. As his engine sucked its last drops of fuel, Martin surged to the lead and a surprise victory.

The moral of this story? It didn't matter how fast Jimmie Johnson's car was when he ran out of gas. It didn't matter how well Greg Biffle had raced for 199 laps because he had nothing to run on for the 200th lap. Mark Martin had the fuel to finish, and he won.

Cash flow for your business is like fuel for a race car. Regardless of how profitable you are, how much your customers love you,

or how sound your strategy is, if you run out of cash, your operations will stop. If you have no source for more cash, your business will cease to exist.

Warren Buffett understands this, and based on the consistent returns of his investments, he has proven to be one of the best allocators of business capital in our time. If you have never read his letters to Berkshire Hathaway shareholders, you should. They are all available online. Not only are they entertaining, but they will quickly reveal his focus on wise cash management. In fact, one of the key business segments in Berkshire Hathaway is insurance because of the amount of capital float (in other words, cash) that it provides for investment.

Since cash flow is so vital to economic survival, you would think that everyone would give it proper attention. But this is not the case. In the first six months following the 2008 financial meltdown, I was talking with a gentleman who used to run a Fortune 500 company and now sits on the boards of several Fortune 500 companies. Amid all the turmoil of that time, he confided that their chief challenge was finding executives who knew how to manage cash flow.

So good for you for investing some time in this course! Whether you are a business owner, an accountant, a banker, a CFO, or an aspiring entrepreneur, you are wise to take this topic so seriously. You might be thinking, "I should already know this stuff." And you might. But regardless of the level of financial training you've had, don't feel foolish for listening to this. The foolish ones are those who take cash flow management for granted, and they're the ones who are losing the lead on the 198th lap. You can't afford for that to happen.

This course is certainly not an exhaustive study, but we *will* cover a broad range of principles related to managing cash flow, as reflected in the Table of Contents on the previous page.

Background

I have over 20 years of experience advising entrepreneurs on the financial aspects of their businesses. Upon graduating from the University of Illinois, I began my career as a CPA. I began delivering CFO advisor services to clients in 2000. After years of refining this work, I created ActionCFO™, a unique process used by CFO advisors to help business owners increase their financial visibility and control without incurring the cost of a full-time CFO.

At about the same time I began serving clients as a CFO advisor, Bill McGuinness published a book entitled *Cash Rules*. The material in Cash Rules for Entrepreneurs draws from both my work as an ActionCFO advisor and Bill's book. Certified ActionCFO advisors continue to teach these concepts to entrepreneurs and business owners, helping them build better businesses by building their mastery of cash flow management.

One more note before we get started… While I recognize that people from many different occupational backgrounds will be reading this, for the sake of simplicity, I will speak throughout as if I'm talking to a business owner. If you are not a business owner, I trust that you can apply the same principles to whatever context is most appropriate for you.

So are you ready to be that third-place driver who ultimately wins the race? Let's get into cash!

Financial Statement Basics

Regardless of your financial background, let's do a brief review of a few financial statement basics. This may seem very elementary to you, but please don't tune out. Sometimes we can become so adept at a skill that we *forget* the basics. If everything I'm about to say is already very familiar to you, great. But more likely than not, you will rediscover an insight that you did not even know you had forgotten.

I will start with five secrets you need to know about financial statements. Then, we will take a quick look at the three basic financial statements and how they work together.

Secret #1:
All accounting and financial statement reporting is driven by one equation:

$$Assets = Liabilities + Equity \text{ (or Net Worth)}$$

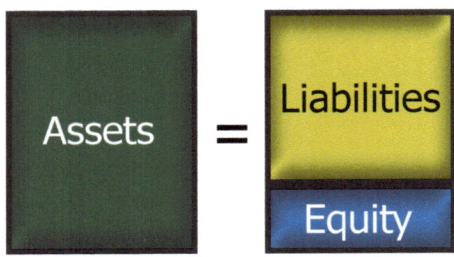

It's really that simple! Accounting is all about making sure that this equation balances.

You must understand this equation to understand the balance sheet – that instant snapshot that shows what is owned and who owns what.

Secret #2:
Accounting and financial statements rely on a lot of estimates. I know, everyone thinks the numbers are "cold, hard facts," but in reality, estimates and judgment calls play a huge role in how financials are reported.

Perhaps you've heard the one about the business owner interviewing candidates for a CFO position. In the final interview, he asks each candidate a simple question, "What is two plus two?" The first two candidates proudly respond with the mathematically correct answer of four. The third candidate

quietly rises from her seat, walks across the room, and closes the door. Upon returning to her seat and with a furtive glance over her shoulder, she whispers, "What would you like it to be?"

Obviously, you can't be *that* flexible with your estimates. But the reality is that it's just not possible – or at least not practical – to get *exact* numbers for every figure. Reasonable estimates can be made based on known facts, and that's commonly understood when looking at a financial statement.

Secret #3

This the difference between accrual and cash basis accounting. These methods differ only in what triggers the recording of a transaction. In accrual based financial statements, the transaction is recorded when the purchase agreement is made. In cash based financial statements, the transaction is recorded when the cash actually changes hands.

Let's walk through an example to illustrate this. (Reference the table on the next page as we go through this.) I have written a book entitled *Before You Hire a CFO* that outlines the Eight Disciplines of Financial Visibility and Control. To make things easy, let's assume that I get $5 in royalties for each book that sells. That's $5 in revenue for each book.

On any given day, I can check to see how many books I've sold, but I don't actually get the cash for those sales until a certain day each month when Amazon sends me a check for all books sold the previous month. For instance, I actually receive the cash for July sales on August 20th. I may have sold books from August 1st through August 19th, but those sales are not reflected in the check I receive on August 20th.

If I'm on accrual basis, I record the income from each sale as it happens even though I don't yet have the cash. You see that represented on your review sheet. Let's pretend the first two sales represent July. On my July statement, I show $10 in revenue for July sales even though I still don't have the cash from these sales in the register. In the first part of August, I sell two more books, and on August 20th, I get the cash for the July sales. I sell one more book before the end of August. Now, on my cumulative statement for July and August, I show $25 in revenue even though I only have $10 in the register.

Let's contrast this with cash basis accounting. If I'm on cash basis, I record the income at the end of the month when the cash rolls in. So on the July statement, since I don't yet have any cash from sales, they might as well have never happened as far as my July statement is concerned. No cash means no

recorded revenue. On August 20th, when I finally receive the cash for July sales, *that's* when I record the revenue, so the cumulative statement for July and August shows $10 in revenue even though I have made a total of five sales which will ultimately net me $25.

So at any given point, my reported income will be different depending on which method I use even though the same amount of money is flowing either way. On the accrual basis, I've made $25 at the end of August. On the cash basis, I've only made $10.

This is extremely important because the monthly income statement is a motion picture of business activity during that month. You cannot mix the methods of recording on the statement. You must consistently use either accrual or cash based recording.

Accrual

	Accounting Revenue	Cash Register
Sale	$5	
Sale	$5	
Monthly Statement	**$10**	**$0**
Sale	$5	
Sale	$5	
Cash Received		$10
Sale	$5	
Monthly Statement	**$25**	**$10**

Cash

	Accounting Revenue	Cash Register
Sale		
Sale		
Monthly Statement	**$0**	**$0**
Sale		
Sale		
Cash Received	$10	$10
Sale		
Monthly Statement	**$10**	**$10**

Secret #4

This the matching principle, a concept that is foundational to sound financial reporting and goes hand-in-hand with accrual basis accounting. It simply means that you record the revenue *and the costs* of an action in the same period. For example, you should not report the revenue of a sale in March but show the costs of that sale in April. They must both be reported in the same month.

Secret #5:

Financial statements are never current. They are historic by nature, providing only a view of *past* performance. Unfortunately for some business owners, by the time they receive their financial statements, it's more like *ancient* information. Fortunately, there are simple disciplines you can

implement to ensure your numbers are still relevant when you see them, which is essential for sound financial decision making.

Having reviewed the five best-kept secrets of the accounting profession, let's talk about financial statements. There are three basic financial statements:

- Balance Sheet,

- Income Statement

- Cash Flow Statement

The balance sheet serves as the bookends. It provides a beginning and ending point by reflecting the balanced accounting equation for your business at a particular point in time. Remember, it shows what is owned and who owns what.

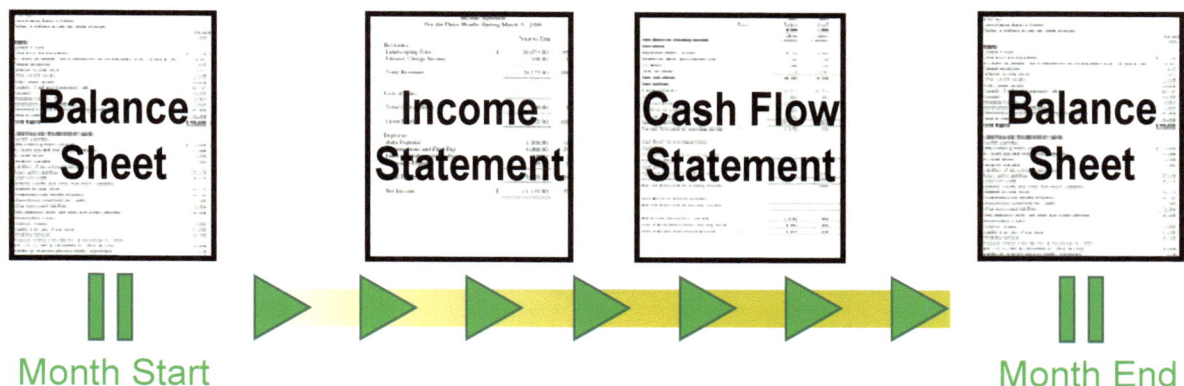

Between these bookends, the income statement and cash flow statement capture the motion. All activity must move through these two statements. It's like freezing the frame on a DVD, hitting 'play,' then freezing the frame again. The freeze frames are on the balance sheet. The income statement and cash flow statement capture what happens in between.

Now, let's walk through a very simple illustration using a financial statement matrix. I will be walking through the "Sample Financial Statement Matrix" shown on the next page.

We begin with our static picture of the balance sheet as it is today. For assets, it shows $700 in cash and $200 in inventory. On the other side of the equation, we have $200 in accounts payable for the

purchase of the inventory from XYZ Company and equity of $700. Now we will simply walk forward with two basic transactions:

1. The business sold on account to ABC Company its entire stock of inventory for $500.

2. The payable to XYZ Company came due and was paid in full – the total $200.

Which of these transactions affected cash? Which affected only the income statement? Selling the inventory on account is an income statement – or non-cash – transaction. In our illustration, we will record $500 of revenue in the income statement column on the line reflecting accounts receivable. With this transaction, we also need to reduce inventory by $200, the full amount sold. This is recorded as a negative $200 in the income statement column on the inventory line.

Since the payable to XYZ Company was related to the inventory, purchased and received in the past, paying this liability is simply a cash flow item. There is no income statement impact. This gets recorded in the cash flow statement column as a negative $200 on the cash line.

When you do the math down, you see that the profit on the income statement is $300 and the cash flow statement shows a negative $200. Doing the math across the matrix, you see the ending balance sheet affected by both the income statement and the cash flow statement. We end with cash of $500 and accounts receivable of $500 due to us from ABC Company. We also end up with equity of $1000.

Sample Financial Statement Matrix

Balance Sheet (beginning)		Income Statement		Cash Flow Statement	Balance Sheet (ending)		
Cash	$ 700			Net CF ($200)	Cash	$	500
Accounts Receivable	$ -	Revenue	$ 500		Accounts Receivable	$	500
Inventory	$ 200	Expenses	$ (200)		Inventory	$	-
Accounts Payable	$ 200			$ (200.00)	Accounts Payable	$	-
Equity	$ 700				Equity (includes profit)	$	1,000
		Profit	$ 300				

5 Sources of Cash

As a business owner, you have five primary sources of cash. The first three are found on the balance sheet; the last two on the income statement. As we go through these, remember the accounting equation: Assets = Liabilities + Equity.

Source #1
Convert an asset to cash. Simply put, sell something. Another possibility is to accelerate collection of Accounts Receivable.

Source #2
Increase liabilities. You might borrow money from the bank or receive inventory from a supplier on credit.

Source #3
Sell equity, such as a stock or a partnership interest for cash.

Source #4
Increase your gross margins. For example, you could negotiate better pricing for volume discounts from suppliers or raise prices without losing revenue. To do the latter, you need to be confident that your customers believe the value you deliver is worth the higher price.

Source #5
Decrease operating expense ratios. For example, outsource a function like telemarketing or find a way to increase sales volume without a related rise in fixed costs.

Each of these five cash sources contains a myriad of options for generating cash.

5 Sources of Cash

1. Sell assets
2. Borrow
3. Sell equity
4. Increase gross margins
5. Decrease operating expense ratios

7 Cash Flow Drivers

Renewable energy is all the rage these days. It was much the same during the "energy crisis" of the 1970s. I remember my parents installing a large solar collector in our side yard that connected to our central air system. It ran for many years, but we eventually scrapped it. By the way, my dad tells me it never paid for itself; it was a bad investment (even after the tax credit)!

Unfortunately, many of today's supposed renewable energy solutions may end up facing the same end as our old solar collector – the scrap yard. Your business, however, has a legitimate source of renewable energy. Do you know what that is? It is cash flow from operations.

Cash flow from operations is exactly what it says: cash flow generated by your basic business operations such as manufacturing and selling a product, delivering a service, or buying products and merchandising them. Whatever you do, if you can do it at a profit, that operating margin provides operating cash flow, a self-sustaining cash source – a *renewable* cash source – for your business. Yes, you can produce enough internal "fuel" to power your business and even grow.

In the book *Cash Rules,* author Bill McGuinness details the 7 Cash Flow Drivers. As an entrepreneur and business owner, you *must* understand these seven cash flow drivers. Other than a few rare exceptions, they control *all* cash flow for *every* business *all* the time.

Cash Driver #1: Sales Growth

We begin with this driver because it is the dominant one. Sales impact every other item on the income statement and balance sheet. Thus, cash flow growth begins with revenue management. You work to manage the volume of revenue you can produce within your current structure *and* you look to grow your top-line which may require adding new structure. (We refer to revenue as "top line" because it is the top line on the income statement.)

One unique aspect of revenue as a cash flow driver is that there is no upper limit. The other six drivers are all limited by the sales volume in which your business operates.

Some of the more mature industries have become very adept at revenue management and built complicated technology and information systems to help wring every possible dollar of revenue out of the market. Airlines, for instance, tightly manage fare price relative to the capacity of a flight. It is unlikely that you paid the same price for your ticket as did the person sitting next to you.

Let's look at four keys to maximizing revenue.

Key #1

Be familiar with the cost structure of your industry. A manufacturer, for example, typically requires high investment in fixed costs such as buildings, equipment, and tools, but generally has the ability to significantly increase volumes within that fixed cost structure. Service companies, on the other hand, typically don't require a large amount of fixed costs up front, but they often have to add more cost structure in order to increase volumes. A machine that runs 1,000 parts per day may also be able to run 100,000 parts per day, but a service technician who currently performs one service call per day may only have the capacity to handle 8 service calls in one day. The service technician costs less up front, but also offers less opportunity for revenue increase.

Key #2

Manage your marketing mix. Peter Drucker said the core of every business is the customer and thus the core function of every business is marketing. This means taking deliberate steps to grow revenue.

Increasing revenue is about more than just increasing the volume of what you currently do; it also includes pricing, selling, expense control, and breadth of product line. Some things that typically create major sales growth include:

- Creating new products or services

- Entering new markets

- Sales-force recruiting and training

- New advertising and promotional campaigns

- New direct marketing tactics

- New inbound marketing strategies

- Improved service levels

- Changes in distribution strategy

- Changes in pricing

Sales Growth Keys

1. Know the cost structure of your industry.

2. Manage your marketing mix.

3. Know your break-even point.

4. Maximize perishable resources.

Changing the mix of these elements can be expensive and difficult. You might get lucky if something grows sales with little effort on your part – but don't count on it.

Key #3

Know your break-even point. This requires an understanding of fixed vs. variable costs and how they relate to your volume or activity levels. You already know the difference between a fixed cost and a variable cost. What may *not* have occurred to you is that some costs have characteristics of *both*. For example:

- I have seen rent agreements in the restaurant and retail industries that are calculated based on revenue thresholds. For a certain range of revenue, the cost is fixed, but once revenue exceeds a certain level, the cost adjusts.

- Another example is paying employees. You might have straight-time costs *and* overtime costs.

- Here's one more: Operations wages are usually considered a variable, yet they include the *fixed* salaries of operations management.

Key #4

Maximize perishable resources. If your inventory is totally perishable, effective resource management is critical. Otherwise, you will pay for a resource that doesn't get used. Examples include hotel rooms, airline seats, and consulting services billed by the hour. If you deal with perishable resources, utilization rate should be one of your smart numbers.

Cash Driver #2: Gross Margin

This cash flow driver is known as the "first of the fundamentals." You need enough gross margin to cover selling, general, and administrative costs, and still have a profit. Arguably, growth in gross margin dollars is more important than growth in revenue. In fact, I have worked with a number of companies who have reaped nice results after shifting their focus from growth in revenue to growth in gross margin and profitability. They did not *abandon* work on the top line, but they shifted their emphasis. We will further explore the growth factor for entrepreneurs later.

Gross margin may be the best financial health indicator in your business because it provides insight into your company's ability to deliver your basic value proposition effectively and efficiently – in other words, profitably. Consistent erosion of gross margin is an early warning that your value proposition is fading in the market. We will talk more about this when we discuss the S-Curve.

There are essentially two ways to improve gross margin. One is to enhance the value of your offering in the eyes of your customers. You might change the product or service itself, change the way it is delivered, or change the way you communicate its value. Opportunities for innovation abound in this area. For example, think about how the internet has enabled shorter delivery channels. In response, many specialty stores have launched web-based retail operations. In the service industry, the internet has streamlined the delivery of intellectual capital, so in addition to delivering a product or service, companies can now develop a training product for what they do and sell it to other industry professionals across the globe.

The second way to improve gross margin is to reduce costs, particularly the costs of making and delivering your product or service. This is rigorous work that typically involves an intense focus on error reduction. It is why businesses aggressively pursue quality control programs such as Lean and Six Sigma. Reducing error generates real dollars.

I'd like to briefly cover two important points relative to gross margin and cost reduction. The first has to do with something we've already talked about: variable vs. fixed costs. Variable costs float with activity levels while fixed costs are added in steps. (See diagram on next page.)

If you don't fully understand the difference between fixed and variable costs, you are susceptible to a common mistake – equating contribution margin to gross margin. Both are important, but they are *not* the same thing. Contribution margin is revenue less the *variable* costs. Gross margin is revenue less fixed *and* variable costs.

The second point relative to gross margin and cost reduction is that the emphasis varies based on your industry.

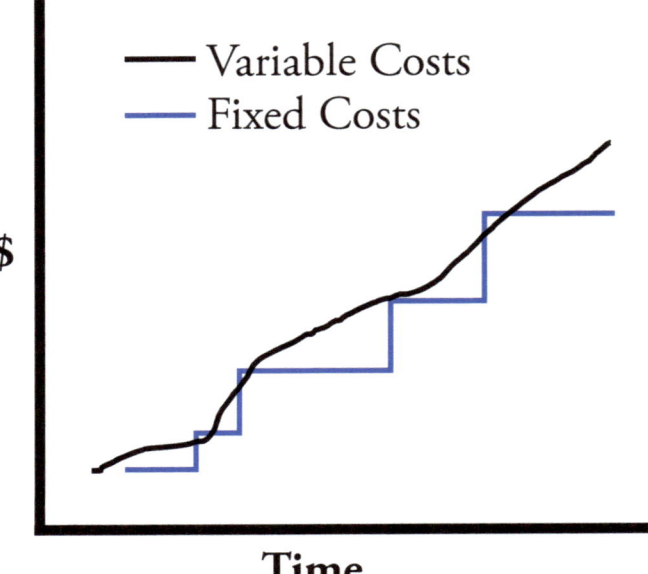

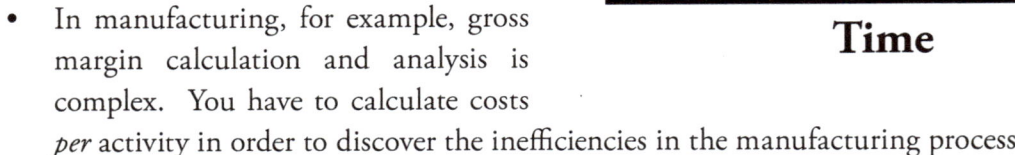

- In manufacturing, for example, gross margin calculation and analysis is complex. You have to calculate costs *per* activity in order to discover the inefficiencies in the manufacturing process.

- In merchandising – that is, distribution and retail – you must focus on managing purchasing and inventory. You must know the right quantities to purchase and when to take markdowns.

- In service businesses, the key is personnel management – talent acquisition, training, and productivity rates, the last of which may be a function of scheduling and routing.

To improve gross margin and contribution margin in your business, analyze them on a product-by-product and customer-by-customer basis. This enables you to pinpoint the specific cost areas to attack. When doing this analysis, you should look at margin *dollars*, not percentages. Many products or services have low gross margin *percentages,* but are great producers of gross margin *dollars.*

Managing gross margin is both art and a science. It may seem prudent to stop all activity on low gross margin dollar producing opportunities and channel those resources into higher gross margin dollar activities. However, two scenarios immediately come to mind where this might not be a good idea:

1. When there is a strategic positioning benefit to offering the full range of products or services.

2. When the market for the higher gross margin dollar producing product or service may be nearing saturation, maturing, or declining. Again, you need to be smart in your refinements. Be sure to balance the short-term with the long-term view.

One way to drive gross margin is to design your motivation and measurement systems around that goal. For example, I've seen many businesses that base incentive compensation on gross margin dollars. Employees can find ways to reduce waste in their particular tasks more easily than they can directly affect corporate overhead costs, so this is a great way to incentivize employees in an area where they have a great deal of control.

Cash Driver #3: Selling, General and Administrative Expenses

Gross margin is the "first of the fundamentals." Selling, general, and administrative expenses is the "second of the fundamentals. " (This is also known as S,G &A or "overhead".) Just like cost of goods sold, this is often a step function. Capacity tends to remain at a fixed level for a given investment, and it largely determines a company's revenue and growth potential. This is why companies will sometimes pursue growth for the sake of "economies of scale." The question is, "How much overhead must I invest to get to the next economy of scale?" Thus, balancing and improving your S, G & A relative to revenue production is very important.

Part of balancing is finding smart ways to reduce costs and gain efficiencies via better training, technology, or process innovations. This applies even when volumes are growing. The chief benefit of cost reduction is a dollar for dollar benefit to the bottom line, as well as a boost in operating cash flow.

When making cuts in down markets, the easiest (and first) cuts are usually those that have the least immediate impact on the success of the firm such as training or marketing, but they are also the cuts that can do the most long-term damage. Cutting S,G & A is hard because it is primarily a "people issue." Compensation and people-related costs comprise the majority of costs that can be cut in a short period of time. Large fixed expenses such as facilities and equipment are mostly set, but people-related expenses can be cut relatively quickly, if necessary. Nobody likes to do that, but sometimes you need to.

The three cash flow drivers we have covered so far (sales growth, gross margin, and S,G & A) are key to determining net profit for your business, and net profit should be the largest contributor to operating cash flow – your renewable energy source. Now, let's continue with the remaining four cash flow drivers.

Cash Driver #4: Accounts Receivable (Swing Factor #1)

This driver won't generate any new cash you haven't already earned through your hard work, but good management of accounts receivable will do one or two things: (1) it will ensure you receive the full cash value of the goods or services you provided to the customer, and (2) it will accelerate your cash flow

stream. The opposite is also true: poor management of accounts receivable results in "lost cash" when you don't receive full value of what was invoiced to the customer. Even if you eventually receive the cash, it pushes the timing of cash receipt further into the future…maybe too far. Accounts receivable may lead to cash, but it can't power your business because it's not fuel. Only cash is fuel.

Accounts receivable is the first and most significant swing factor because getting paid by the customer is paramount. In offering credit to a customer, you make four assumptions: (1) the customer is willing to pay, (2) the customer is able to pay, (3) the customer's willingness to pay won't fail before the order is shipped or payment is due, and (4) the customer's ability to pay won't fail by the time the order is shipped or payment is due.

You should really view accounts receivable based on the number of days cash is tied up in it. This is known as Days Sales Outstanding, or DSO – the average number of days it takes to collect your receivables after providing the goods or services and invoicing the customer.

$$DSO = 365 \left/ \frac{Revenue}{Avg.\ Accts.\ Receivable\ Outstanding} \right.$$

Set up simple policies to help your business convert receivables to cash more quickly and efficiently. Here are a few things to think about as you do this.

1. Decide when you and/or your senior management should become involved in the collection effort.

2. Be mindful of the marketing aspect of accounts receivable. The delinquent customer is still a customer, so your staff should treat him as a valued customer who is temporarily behind. This approach will preserve your business relationships in spite of challenging collection issues.

3. Weekly cash flow forecasting is one of the best ways to stay on top of receivables. Each week, review accounts receivable to find customers from whom you expected payment the previous week. This will quickly identify potential problem areas for follow-up, including those where senior management should get involved. We will go into more detail on this discipline later.

Before moving on from this cash flow driver, let's talk about factoring. Factoring allows businesses to sell their accounts receivable in advance for some discount off of the face value of the receivable. This is an expensive way to accelerate cash flow; the annualized cost of factoring tends to be very high relative to the cost of bank financing or other debt. Therefore, you should not factor unless you cannot get the cash you need from any other source. If your situation requires factoring, compare the cost of factoring to the additional contribution margin you can generate with the extra cash before moving ahead.

There is one more often overlooked benefit of factoring. Accounts receivable must be carried on your books, but factoring outsources the accounts receivable function. This makes the decision of whether or not to factor about more than the cost of money – it's about how to reduce S, G & A expenses.

Cash Driver #5: Inventory (Swing Factor #2)

Inventory is most applicable to manufacturing and merchandising businesses. Again, this is a swing factor because while it doesn't necessarily generate new cash, it can accelerate the flow of cash back into the business for use in funding further sales growth. Pay attention to the following four items:

1. Inventory days should be a prime motivator for your business – not just overall, but product by product. The formula for Days Inventory Outstanding is:

$$DIO = 365 / \frac{COGS}{Avg.\ Inventory}$$

2. Understand the concept of just-in-time (or pull vs. push). Pull is when market demand determines the quantity and speed of your production. You keep inventory levels only at the level required by the customer for the next short period of time instead of stockpiling larger quantities of inventory as a buffer in the supply chain. The downside of this is that the absence of a buffer in the supply chain can cost you when emergencies inevitably happen.

3. Fine-tune your purchasing and inventory management.

4. Make sure you understand the related costs of inventory: ordering costs, carrying costs, and cost of running out of stock. Carrying costs are the largest of the three and include several key components: financial costs (such as capital, taxes and insurance), physical costs (such as storage and handling), and risk costs (such as deterioration, pilferage, and obsolescence).

Inventory management is most applicable to manufacturing and merchandising businesses, but it can also apply to service and professional businesses. Human resources and incomplete development projects can be treated as inventory. When employees are working on a project, they can't generate revenue until the project is completed – just like product sitting on a shelf can't generate revenue until it is sold. In both cases, you're spending real dollars.

Cash Driver#6: Accounts Payable (Swing Factor #3)

Accounts payable is similar to the inventory swing factor in that it is most applicable to manufacturing and merchandising businesses. That said, all businesses may find buying on credit to be a way of matching the cash flow reality. For example, if you are developing a new product or service, paying cash later for development costs will shorten the time until cash flows in from selling the same offering.

Setting disciplined policies around payables and enforcing them makes good sense. Match the documentation throughout your financial system and periodically review payables, terms for various vendors, and accrued expenses. For instance, supplier discounts for early payment are often the best available return on investment, so you want to make sure you capitalize on those. Through it all, you want to maximize DPO (Days Payables Outstanding). In other words, hold off paying for as long as possible.

$$DPO = 365 \; / \; \frac{Purchases}{Avg. \; Accts. \; Payable \; Outstanding}$$

I'd like to review three often overlooked caveats regarding accounts payable management:

1. Just because a supplier offers a discount for early payment does not mean you should take it. What if you could put that cash to more productive use in other parts of your business? You may be able to generate greater contribution margin than the early payment discount return.

2. Businesses accustomed to buying on credit sometimes overlook purchase discounts such as buying office supply items at retail discounters rather than on credit with delivery.

3. Be careful stretching payables terms (paying vendors in 45 or 60 days instead of the standard 30 days, for example). If you always take as much rope as the supplier permits, you may not find any slack left when you really need it. Large businesses are notorious for abusing this practice. If you deal with any of them in your business, you know what I'm talking about.

That completes the three swing factor cash flow drivers – accounts receivable, inventory, and accounts payable. One final comment on all of them: remember that if revenue management and the fundamentals (gross margin and S, G & A) are deteriorating, you can usually tighten the swing factors a bit to create some breathing room while you get them back on track. The fundamentals, however, are *fundamental*, so your opportunity to correct them is finite.

Cash Driver #7 – Capital Expenditures (CAPEX)

Capital expenditures greatly impact cash flow because they are typically large dollar amounts. They cover non-expendable fixed assets like equipment, software, vehicles, buildings, etc. Businesses typically have to obtain outside financing for this.

I'd like to touch on four important items relative to CAPEX:

1. Fixed assets and revenue are related. Do you understand what increase in asset levels will be required for a given increase in revenue in your business?

2. Depreciation is not cash flow. It is simply an estimate of the expenditure for the asset spread out over its useful life. Companies sometimes take advantage of the latitude this provides in estimating what to record on the financial statements. Further complicating the estimation of depreciation is the tax code which has strict rules covering the useful lives of certain fixed assets but then provides numerous acceleration provisions as incentives for companies to purchase capital goods. This, of course, creates a fairly wide range of judgment for estimating depreciation costs, opening the door for dubious behaviors. For example, publicly traded companies looking to attract investors might change the estimation method to show an increase in profitability, while privately held businesses looking to avoid taxes want to show a decrease in profitability.

3. Companies, industries, and entire economies can get caught in technological or economic shifts. A business may have the best available technology today, but when that technology becomes outdated, they must choose between competing with more of their current equipment or scrapping their capital investments to start over. For example, think about the edge enjoyed by developing countries who go from no phone lines to today's best cellular technology while more developed countries have 100 years of old line infrastructure to deal with.

4. Financing is a key lubricant to CAPEX capability for most businesses. We won't go into great detail on financing options for entrepreneurs, but note that one such option, – leasing – may allow you to have an obligation that does not appear on the balance sheet. Operating leases are expensed as paid while financing leases are set on the balance sheet at the present value of their total liability (like a loan).

7 Cash Flow Drivers

1. Sales Growth
2. Gross Margin
3. Selling, General & Administrative Expenses (S,G&A)
4. Accounts Receivable (Swing Factor #1)
5. Inventory (Swing Factor #2)
6. Accounts Payable (Swing Factor #3)
7. Capital Expenditures (CAPEX)

Working Capital and the Cash Conversion Cycle

Working capital and the cash conversion cycle tie directly to the three swing factor cash flow drivers (accounts receivable, inventory and accounts payable).

Working capital is simply current assets less current liabilities.

$$\text{Working Capital} = \text{Current Assets} - \text{Current Liabilities}$$

Obviously, the largest components of working capital are accounts receivable, inventory, and accounts payable. You understand that there is a cost to having cash tied up in accounts receivable and inventory – whether that is due to financing costs or simply not being able to aggressively invest in growth. You also understand that your capital position is helped by the amount you purchase on credit. The cash conversion cycle pulls all of this together to help entrepreneurs manage this important side of their businesses.

The formula for Cash Conversion Cycle is:

$$\text{Cash Conversion Cycle (CCC)} = \text{DIO} + \text{DSO} - \text{DPO}$$

An improving Cash Conversion Cycle results when you improve the turn-around of inventory and collect accounts receivables more quickly (in other words, decrease Days Inventory Outstanding and Days Sales Outstanding).

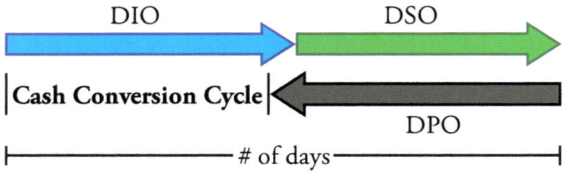

A deteriorating Cash Conversion Cycle results when inventory turns and accounts receivables collections are stretching out.

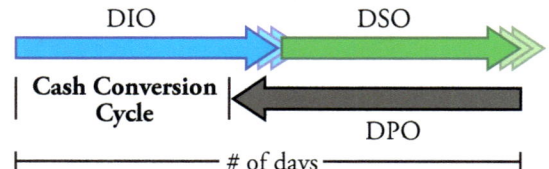

You get a negative Cash Conversion Cycle when you receive cash from customers before you need to pay vendors for that inventory. Yes, that is possible. Dell is the poster child for this. They typically collect cash on average 40 days before they pay for inventory.

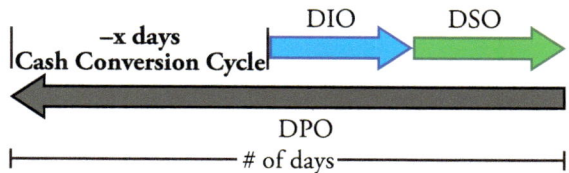

Earlier, I said that if revenue management and your fundamental cash flow drivers (which are gross margin and S, G & A) are weakening, you can help cash flow by tightening up on the swing factors. Even better, if your revenue management and fundamentals are sound, tightening up on the swing factors does three more things for you:

1. It frees up cash flow which can be used to reduce debt, distribute to owners, or fund even greater growth.

2. It improves your profitability by saving on financing costs (assuming you have outside financing in place for working capital).

3. It improves your return on invested capital.

The cash conversion cycle is a measure of operating efficiency. It answers the question, "How quickly does the business take cash, produce something of value, sell it for a profit, and convert it back to cash?"

Companies can accelerate their cash conversion cycle in several ways:

- In project-based industries (construction, for instance), companies commonly require some percentage of the payment up front as well as progress payments at the completion of certain stages of the job. This provides the working capital needed to fund the work along the way. Such a business can increase its cash conversion cycle by increasing the up-front percentage it requires. For example, on a $250,000 project, increasing the up-front charge from 25% to 40% translates to $37,500 more in working capital.

- Some professional services accelerate the CCC by working on a retainer instead of hourly fees.

- Many businesses offer a small discount to customers who pay early.

- Some companies (like Dell) are able to receive payment from customers before even ordering the parts to manufacture the product.

Like Dell, Walmart is well known for significantly improving its cash conversion cycle. Between 2000 and 2004, its cash conversion cycle went from 22 days to 15 days. With Walmart's large volumes, this equated to large dollars – $4 billion of working capital.

Let's look at how Dell and Walmart approached this. For both, Days Sales Outstanding was relatively short (consumer credit card sales are about 3 - 4 days outstanding) so they began by focusing on the inventory swing factor. Dell established a frequent rhythm of meetings and incentives to align the sales plan and commissions to the production plan. Walmart focused on supplier management and logistics. At some point, both achieved a position in their industries where they had enough leverage with vendors to turn the Days Payable Outstanding component further in their favor.

The Growth Factor

You can't talk to entrepreneurs and not talk about the growth factor. Entrepreneurs want to grow their businesses. Frankly, the no-growth choice is seldom an option except perhaps with a one-person operation or closely-held family business that doesn't expect to continue beyond the first generation.

The allure of growth for entrepreneurs, however, is akin to the enchantment of the Sirens' song for Odysseus in Homer's Odyssey. The Sirens were known for luring men to their death with their beautiful songs. Odysseus had been warned of this, so he ordered his men ahead of time to tie him to the ship's mast (after he had stuffed all of their ears) to keep from following the Sirens' song.

Similarly, the temptation to grow *at all costs* is powerful, requiring foresight and discipline to avoid succumbing. Of course, growth is not necessarily bad; in fact, growth is important to keep individuals and businesses from stagnating. The key is to recognize that "getting larger" or "moving faster" does not automatically mean "growth." Entrepreneurs endanger their organizations when "larger" becomes

the target rather than the natural result of pursuing the target. A much better objective is growth in value – the value of what is provided to the customer and the financial value of the business. Growth sounds so good, but the undisciplined pursuit of growth can lead your business to its "death."

Bill McGuinness says it well in *Cash Rules*. For entrepreneurs, the idea of sales-volume growth has been so ingrained in their heads (as well it should be) that it often combines with some erroneous logic. When the company needs more cash, they think, "Let's sell lots of stuff, customers will give us money, and the cash problem will go away." But this does not always work. Why? Because growth consumes cash.

Look at the graphic below. See how cash lags revenue? Cash is invested in people and materials and something is delivered to the customer. If you sell on credit, as most businesses do, you carry accounts receivable. The customer sends you the cash 30, 45 or even 60 days later. If you accelerate the revenue curve, (that is, you sell more), you increase the amount of receivables you must fund.

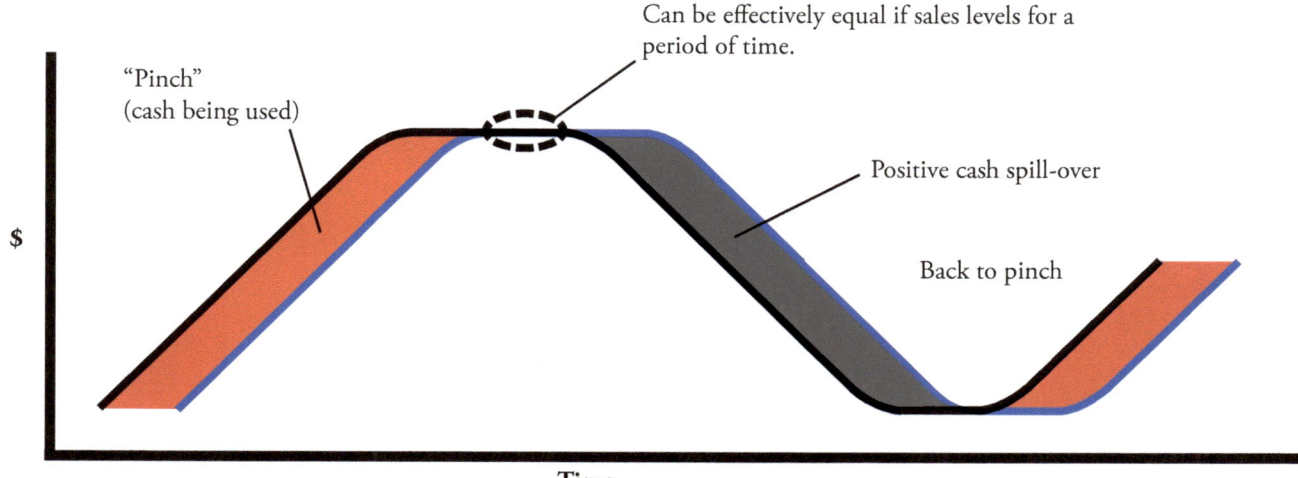

Here are two more important perspectives related to growth and cash flow. First, the only thing worse than no growth is poorly planned growth. Second, while you may not run out of cash as your business grows, you will be less efficient in its use (due to necessary administrative additions) and/or riskier with your financial structure – maybe exposing yourself to an increased leverage ratio.

How quickly should you grow? This is one question for which there is a formula:

$$\text{Sustainable Growth Rate} = \text{Net Income} / (\text{Net Worth} - \text{Net Income})$$

Essentially, the Sustainable Growth Rate measures return on equity. **Please note**: this formula represents a <u>steady-state business.</u> It assumes no change in leverage ratio, constant net profit margins, constant proportion of profits retained for investment or paid as dividends, and no change in the return on assets.

If growth exceeds this rate, the extra cash must come from at least one of five sources:

1. Reducing the percentage of profit paid in dividends

2. Borrowing proportionally more than in the past

3. Increasing net margins by reducing unit costs – that is, getting more economies of scale on overhead expenses

4. Selling at a higher price without losing volume

5. Improving asset efficiency – that is, increasing assets at a rate slower than sales growth.

The sustainable growth rate is based on accrual profit, which is a little different than cash profit. Because of this, I recommend that you determine the sustainable growth rate for your business in conjunction with a full financial statement projection – balance sheet, income statement and cash flow statements. This will provide you with a clearer view of the cash picture.

So again, how quickly should you grow? Ideally, you want to push your actual growth rate right up to the level of the sustainable growth rate. This is management's responsibility.

As a brief aside, I'd like to address an important non-financial consideration relative to growth. Having worked with many organizations as an advisor on strategic issues, I am a firm believer in Packard's Law (so named after Dave Packard, cofounder of Hewlett Packard). Packard's Law says that you can only grow as fast as you can bring the right people into your organization. Many organizations have dollars to grow, but they can't leverage the full financial returns due to inadequate talent. Don't waste your

time and money with growth until you have the right people on board.

Now for a warning: *don't get lulled to sleep by downturns in the market.* I showed earlier how growth consumes cash. It logically follows that a business can actually see an influx of cash during a period of decline. Look at the graphic on page 23 again. See what happens to cash when revenue declines? If growth stops for awhile, cash flow catches up. Cash is coming into the business at essentially the same pace as new sales. When revenue declines, cash continues to flow into the business at the pace of the higher revenue volume a few months prior. This is a budding problem, however, because more cash is coming in than is being funded in receivables from new sales.

I call this the "great cash spill-over," and it occurs whenever revenue volumes decline. Beware of the "great cash spill-over," because it doesn't last forever, and it lulls many entrepreneurs to sleep. Don't let this happen to you.

Now that you understand the revenue/cash curve, you will see the "great cash spill-over" as a warning sign of a coming cash crunch. When this happens, make the necessary adjustments to be *profitable* at lower volumes as quickly as possible. You must do more than just minimize losses or get to break-even or else – well, you'll be like Jimmie Johnson running out of fuel two laps from the finish line. One minute you think you're winning, the next minute you've finished near the back of the pack.

By the way, did you know that the most dangerous time in a recession is when it ends? That's right. The time that should worry you most is the *end* of a recession. The reason has everything to do with cash. When a company uses up its reserves during a down market, it may not have enough cash to grow when the market rebounds. Remember? Growth consumes cash. Even if you have the cash (the fuel) to sustain your business during a period of break-even or losses, the longer that time goes, the less likely you are to have enough fuel to power a comeback. As sales grow, the receivables, payroll, inventories, and other expenses will likely *precede* any infusion of cash by 30, 60, or even 90 days. Again, you can see this on the graphic on page 23.

The Innovation Curve

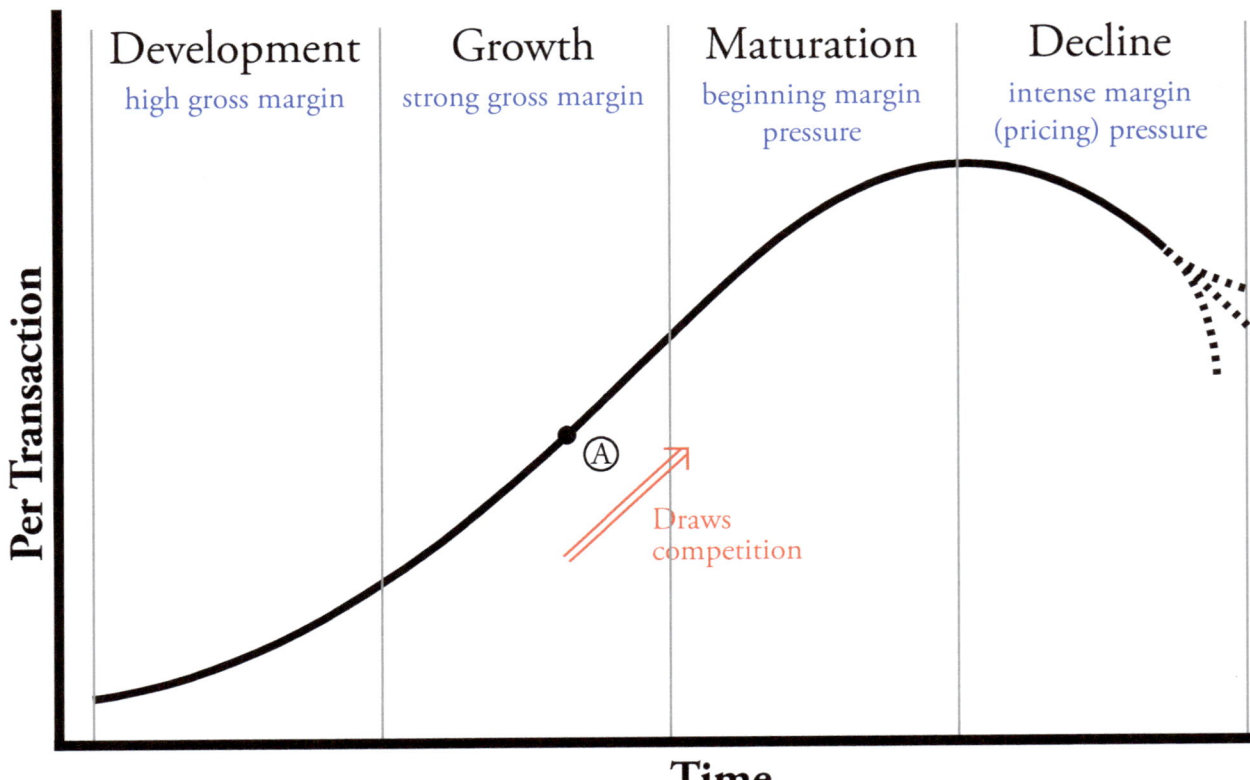

(A) Inflection Point: rate of growth increases before and decreases after.

Look at the diagram above. This illustration is simply known as the S-Curve or Innovation Curve. The x-axis is time. We'll label the y-axis as "per transaction" – it might be revenue per transaction or profit per transaction. It could also represent production volume. This curve highlights four distinct phases in the life cycle of an innovation, whether that's a product, service offering, technology, business model, etc.

The first phase is the development phase. In the early stages of the innovation, investment typically exceeds return, but you see real potential for high gross margin percentages as a few early adopters begin using the product.

The second phase is growth. The innovation is rapidly adopted by the market. Your business enjoys strong growth in revenue and profits. Gross margins are strong. Your growth rate increases early and decreases late, but growth continues throughout.

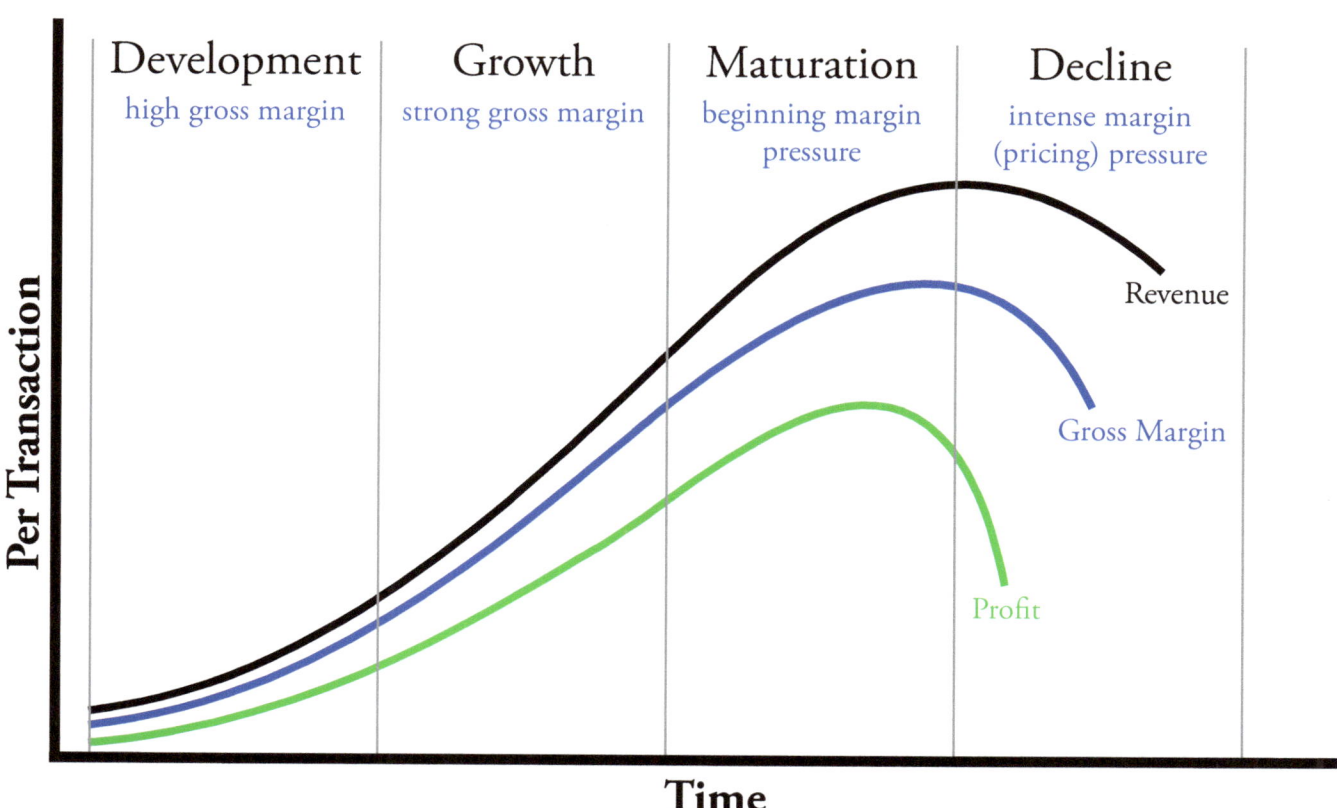

As the growth rate slows to a certain level, you enter the third phase – maturity. Your business is enjoying the highest revenue and profits from the innovation, but gross margins begin to feel some pressure. Why? As you moved up the growth curve, your innovation attracted competition. Key knowledge became commonplace giving competitors a chance to catch up or even pass you on the curve. Perhaps new innovations have even disrupted the curve.

Here's an example. In the 1990s, industrial robot programming was a specialized area of knowledge requiring skilled programmers to invest a lot of time with each robot. In the 2000s, this specialized knowledge was increasingly hard-coded into the robots' basic functionality and the programming interface become more and more intuitive. This has shifted the balance of power away from the specialized programmers as less skilled programmers can now do tasks they could not do before. For a given robot, a specialized programmer may be needed for only 20 hours instead of 60 hours.

Sometimes we call this commoditization, the phenomenon where a once unique innovation now has many similar alternatives. The only competitive differentiator remaining is price.

The fourth stage on the S-Curve is decline. As gross margin pressure intensifies, the question is not if

you will decline, but how quickly…unless you innovate again.

Following are a few insights to help you apply the S-Curve to your situation.

Insight #1

When talking about the gross margin cash flow driver, I noted that gross margin might be the best leading indicator of the health of your position in the market. This is what happens at the top of the curve as the innovation moves from maturity to decline. Gross margin pressure intensifies, pushing gross margins lower. The delivery method of the offering probably won't work for long without some adjustments. Remember the two primary ways to maintain or increase your gross margin? You can either enhance the value proposition of your offering in the eyes of your customers, or reduce the costs of making or delivering the product or service.

Insight #2

If you are past the inflection point of the curve, you should look for ways to reinvest the profit dollars "under the curve" back into new innovations that either renew and extend your existing curve, build new curves, or, at a minimum, slow the decline of your existing curve. (See the diagram below.)

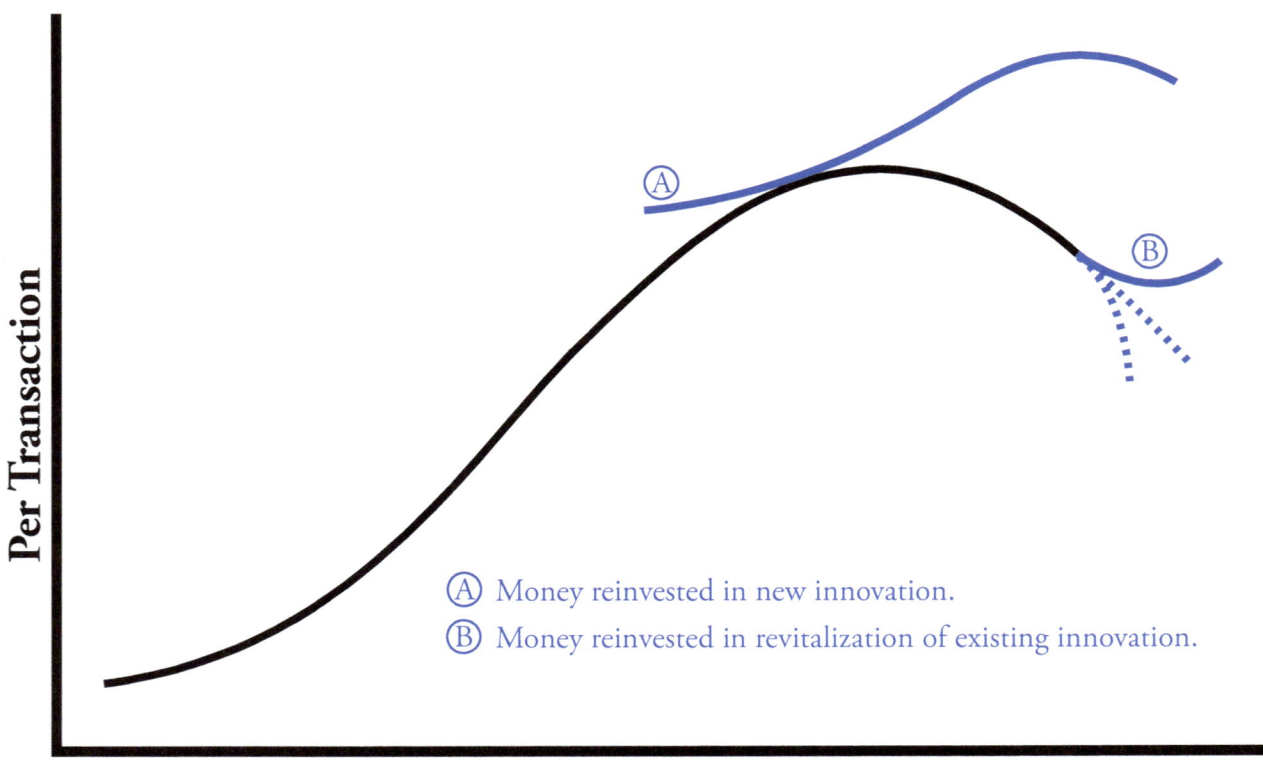

Ⓐ Money reinvested in new innovation.
Ⓑ Money reinvested in revitalization of existing innovation.

Insight #3

Experience will help you. We could draw another curve demonstrating how costs decrease per transaction as experience increases. The more you do something, the more proficient and efficient you become.

Insight #4

Your position on the curve will determine how you need to manage. Some businesses choose to play in only certain phases of the curve because the business structure and management requirements are so different for each. Please contact me if you would like to discuss this further.

Insight #5

Never stop innovating! Many businesses try to ride an innovation curve too far and fail to reinvest money in future innovation.

Insight #6

Maximizing dollars out of an existing innovation is a challenge for entrepreneurs. Just as an innovation curve can be ridden too long, some entrepreneurs jump too quickly to new innovations. This can frustrate employees with too much change, and it might also leave money on the table. You need to ride the innovation curve long enough to maximize the return on investment. If you'd rather move to something else, perhaps you can sell the innovation to someone who wants to play that role.

In conclusion, spend some more time studying the S-Curve and thinking about its practical applications for your business. Understanding the lifecycle of an innovation is very important for entrepreneurs when making strategic and financial decisions.

The Value Vector

This is where we begin tying the cash flow drivers to decisions that drive the value of a business. Building business value is where financial management and strategy most closely align. To maximize the value of your business, you need to understand both the past financial performance and the future possibilities of your economic engine.

Value is the *future* return on invested capital. The technical process to determine value is called Discounted Cash Flow and consists of two components: risk and operating cash flow. You must understand the interaction and the variable drivers of these two components, for that is the only way to maximize value and yield the highest *future* return on invested capital and talent.

Let's begin by looking at a simple illustration of how value is determined, something we call the Value Vector. See the illustration to the right.

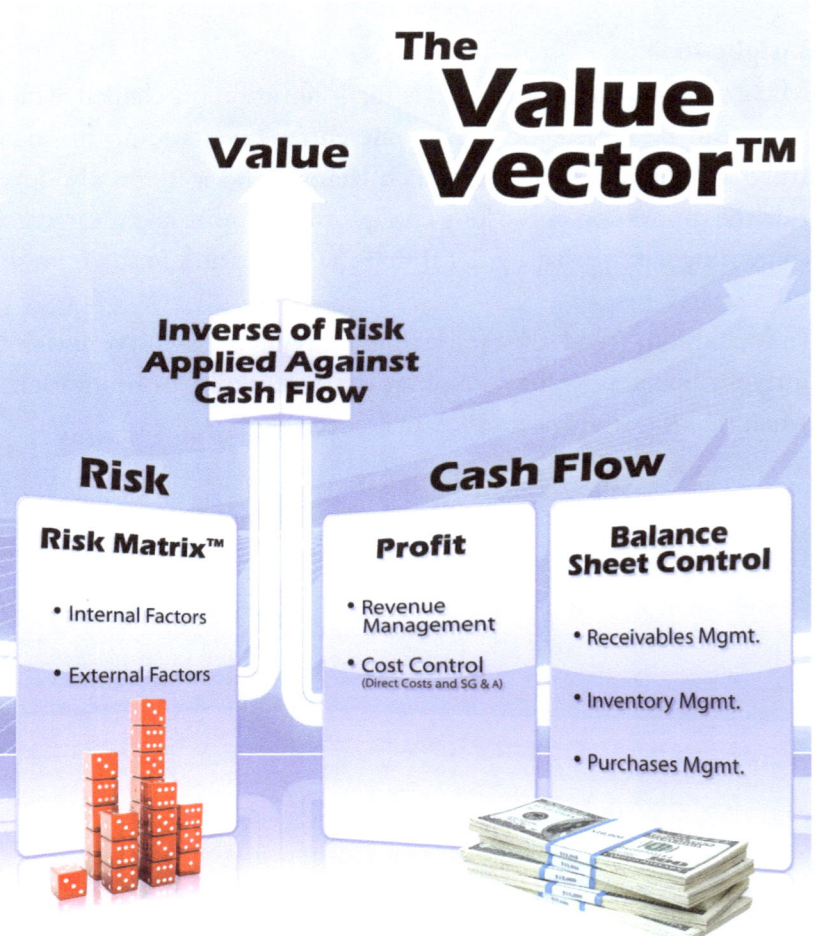

Value is simply risk applied to cash flow. Every business has a certain risk assigned to its future performance. You can think of *risk* as the return investors expect relative to other possible investments. For example, investment in a business is considered more risky than investment in government bonds. Similarly, investment in a small business is generally considered more risky than investment in a large business.

In addition to risk characteristics, every business has an expected future operating cash flow.

Different proxies of operating cash flow may be used in different situations, such as EBITDA (earnings before interest, taxes, depreciation and amortization) or operating income (net income before miscellaneous or unusual expenses). Value for any given business is simply the inverse of the risk multiplied by the expected future operating cash flow.

If a potential investor judges a business to have a risk level that requires a 25% return, and this business has an expected annual average operating cash flow of $100,000, the value of that business would be the inverse of 25%, which is 4, times $100,000 for a value of $400,000. In this example, the expected 25% return converts to a four times *multiple*. A three times multiple would yield a lower value due to a higher perceived risk by the investor who would need to return 33% on the investment. Similarly, if the investor's perceived risk is lower, maybe only expecting a 20% return, then it would be a five times multiple and yield a higher value for the business. In short, lowering the risk and/or increasing the operating cash flow increases the company's value. Raising the risk and/or decreasing the operating cash flow decreases the company's value.

Risk Level: 25% return required

Operating Cash Flow: $100,000

Value: (1/25%) x $100,000 = $400,000

Who determines the risk level and expected cash flow, and thus the value, of a business? Only a potential buyer can make that determination. Like any free-market transaction, it all depends on what someone is willing to pay.

Each of the primary factors in determining value – risk and operating cash flow – have multiple drivers that create a unique interplay in any business. Let's consider those drivers in more detail.

Variable Drivers of Risk
The variable drivers of risk fall into two simple categories: internal risk factors and external risk factors. Internal risk factors include:

- Strength of the management team
- Diversity of the customer base

- Diversity of the revenue stream

- Revenue growth rate relative to industry growth rate

- Reliance on one or two key people

- Size relative to competitors

External risk factors include:

- State of the industry (is it in the growth, maturity or decline phase?)

- Government regulation within the industry

- Competitive environment (are there low or high barriers to entry?)

- Technology advances

- Global business environment

- Macroeconomic factors such as interest rates and money availability

These lists are far from comprehensive, but they provide a sampling of the types of risk characteristics investors consider. Like snowflakes, no two businesses are alike. No two businesses have the same risk complexion, and potential buyers will assess risk differently based on their present situations. Indeed, the value of a business complies with the old saying: "beauty is in the eye of the beholder."

To study this topic further, I recommend Tom McKaskill's book *Selling Your Business For a Premium*. It discusses how to identify buyers with the best "risk fit" to achieve the highest possible value for your business.

Variable Drivers of Operating Cash Flow
The variable drivers of operating cash flow fall into two categories: profit drivers and balance sheet control drivers.

The profit driver category includes revenue management and cost control. Revenue management ties back to value proposition pricing and promotion of a product or service, as well as systems to determine different prices for different customers based on quantity discounts or other factors. For example, airline companies use complex systems to maximize revenue across a broad range of customer needs. (We talked about this when we discussed the first cash flow driver.)

Cost control includes both direct costs (cost of goods sold) and all other costs, including S,G & A

expenses. Clearly, a business cannot focus solely on cost control at the expense of revenue growth, but cost control plays a key role in maximizing operating cash flow. Every dollar in revenue only yields the contribution margin of that dollar to cash flow, but every dollar in cost savings yields that full dollar to cash flow. Therefore, time focused on cost control is time well spent.

In many respects, cost control is directly related to quality. For instance, a 4% error rate will consume 54% of the company's resources (time, money, and creative energy). The staggering "cost of quality" is well documented, and you can study it with programs like Six Sigma and Lean Manufacturing.

The balance sheet control driver category includes three distinct variable drivers: receivables management, inventory management, and purchasing management, each of which directly impacts operating cash flow. For instance, your business might implement a collection and accounts receivable review process that reduces average days outstanding of accounts receivable from 60 to 45 days.

How to Increase the Value of Your Business
Decreasing risk factors and increasing operating cash flow simultaneously increases business value. Sometimes, however, you must focus more heavily on one or the other. With no change to risk factors, improving cash flow will increase the value of your business. Similarly, your business might have no significant increase in cash flow, yet increase its value simply by mitigating one or more risk factors.

For example, if 50% of your revenue comes from one customer, you likely need to diversify your customer base. If no more than 10% of your revenue comes from any one customer while maintaining the same operating cash flow, your business will be perceived as less risky and therefore more valuable to a potential purchaser. Why? You have lowered the risk of a large financial impact to the future operating cash flow stream if you lose a customer.

In summary, the best way to increase the value of your business is to implement strategic initiatives that both mitigate risk and increase operating cash flow.

Let's go back to the S-curve for a minute in the context of business value determination. A business is valued based on the dollars you can reasonably expect to:

1. Press out of the innovation over time (the remaining dollars available under the curve), or
2. Build out of a new innovation curve that jumps off of the existing curve. (Perhaps the business is working on a promising innovation or the purchaser can leverage his own innovation to build a new curve.) Reference the diagram on the next page.

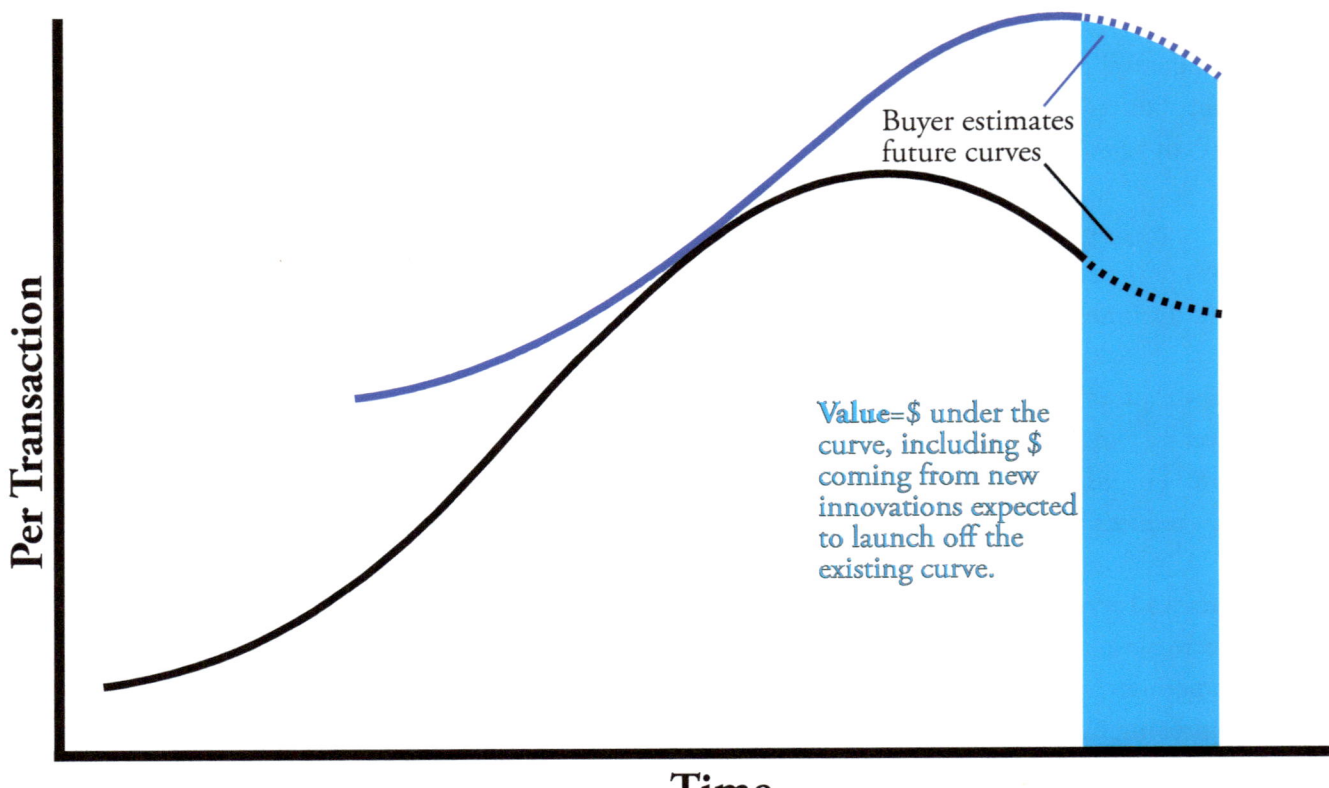

In either case, it comes down to the future expected dollars available under the curve(s). This is illustrated above.

If you're like most people, you like shortcuts. Gleaning from the wisdom of people more experienced and wiser than you is a great shortcut. Here are Seven Points of Wisdom from Bill McGuinness, author of *Cash Rules*, related to driving value-building disciplines in your business.

Wisdom Point #1

Entrepreneurs often understand that business value is more closely related to cash flow than earnings. They just aren't always good at tracking and living by it.

Wisdom Point #2

Conserving equity by eliminating excess payments to owners allows you to build a stronger capital base from which to grow. This accelerated growth is less risky growth when the business is not over-leveraged.

Wisdom Point #3

One risk of eliminating stockholder payouts is the temptation to overpay for acquisitions or expansions. In this situation, entrepreneurs don't tend to be as stingy with their capital resources.

Wisdom Point #4

If no internal investment alternatives or acquisitions make sense, a company can always buy back its own stock before paying dividends (if the stock is in the public market or there are multiple owners in the business), thereby decreasing the number of outstanding shares – owners – of the business.

Wisdom Point #5

Paying a dividend to owners is often an unintended acknowledgement by management that it doesn't have the creativity to use the cash wisely in the business. Essentially, management has returned it to shareholders so they can spend or invest it elsewhere. This same thought has been expressed by Peter Drucker, Warren Buffett, and others.

Wisdom Point #6

It is rare to not find good internal investment opportunities if you take the time and trouble to look.

Wisdom Point #7

When doing an acquisition, make sure the deal improves not only cash flow but the entire value equation. Will the acquisition drive the company's flywheel? In other words, does it fit the passion, "best in the world" capability, and economic engine criteria of the company's Hedgehog Concept? If not, it is unlikely to increase the overall value equation for the business. (If you're not familiar with the Hedgehog Concept, read Chapter 5 of *Good to Great* by Jim Collins.)

The Four Bottom Lines

What's the bottom line? It's net profit, right? Well, yes, that's the correct answer. But the *question* is wrong. It should be: What are the bottom line**s**? You see, net profit is only one of *four* bottom lines which indicate the true financial performance of a company; in fact, it's not even the most important of the four.

The four bottom lines that a business owner must fully understand and monitor are:

- Return on Invested Capital

- Net Profit

- Operating Cash Flow

- Profit Per Employee

Like all metrics, each of these has inherent limitations and weaknesses, but as a package, they provide a complete view of "bottom line performance" with which to evaluate the health of the business.

Remember: all bottom lines are lagging indicators, measuring past performance. Past performance does not determine future success. However, understanding the variables for each of these metrics can help you make decisions that will move them in a positive direction.

Let's take a look at each of these bottom lines. (They are summarized on the next page.)

Return on Invested Capital

If I had to pick the most important of the four bottom lines, this would probably be it. This measure demonstrates how successfully the business enterprise turns capital into profit. In other words, it measures how effectively the company uses its money. After all, the primary financial reason for a business to exist is to return profit to investors and lenders. To be considered a strong performer, a business must at least yield a return higher than its cost of capital.

Look at the denominator of this formula. It is based on the balance sheet, but with net profit as the prime input of the numerator, this measure is equally affected by revenue and expenses.

Return on invested capital is very useful when comparing the financial performance of different businesses, whether within or across industries. Every company generates different revenue, profit,

The Four Bottom Lines

#1: Return On Invested Capital

Demonstrates how successfully the business enterprise converts capital to profit.

$$\frac{\text{Net Profit} + \text{Interest} + \text{Amortization}}{\text{Total Assets} - \text{Excess Cash} - \text{Non-Interest-Bearing Current Liabilities}}$$

Limitations:
- Does not measure cash flow.
- Can be manipulated.
- Most difficult bottom line to measure.

How efficiently are you operating regardless of revenue, profit, or cash flow levels?

#2: Net Profit

Measures the economic reality of a value proposition over time.

Revenue - Operating Expenses

Limitations:
- Does not reveal the real cash situation.
- Can be manipulated.

Do your present activities actually make money?

Are you watching all four?

#3: Operating Cash Flow

Measures how much cash is generated by business operations.

Cash flow excluding cash items related to capital investments, investors, or lenders.

Limitations:
- Can be manipulated.
- Can be increased at the expense of profit.

Can you expect to survive? Profits don't matter if you don't have any cash.

#4: Profit Per Employee

Measures the returns on talent in addition to capital.

$$\frac{\text{Net Profit}}{\text{\# Full-Time Equivalent Employees}}$$

Limitations:
- Does not reveal the real cash situation.
- Abstract
- Can be manipulated.

Can you convert raw talent into profits?

and cash flow levels, but *return on invested capital* provides an equalizing measure of how effectively companies produce profit from a given base of resources.

I mentioned earlier that each bottom line has inherent limitations. The limitations of *return on invested capital* include:

- It does not measure cash flow.

- It can be easily manipulated by accounting methods.

- It is more difficult to measure than the other three bottom line measurements.

Net Profit

Here's the one you're all familiar with. *Net Profit* measures the economic reality of a value proposition over time. In other words, is the customer willing to pay more for the product or service than it costs the business to produce and deliver it? If so, the business will generate a net profit. This metric is calculated by deducting all operating expenses from total revenue. This metric is commonly presented in actual dollars as well as percent of revenue (for instance, $50,000 in profit or 6.8% of revenue for the month).

To fully understand *net profit*, review the accrual basis and matching principle from earlier in this course.

The inherent limitations of *net profit* include:

- It does not reveal the real cash situation since it focuses on the promise and agreement part of a business transaction.

- It is an abstract measure because it comes from the income statement and can be manipulated with different accounting methods.

Operating Cash Flow

As you know, cash flow for a business is like fuel for a vehicle; a business can operate for awhile at a net loss, but it cannot operate one day without cash. Thus, it is imperative that you track *operating cash flow* – the amount of cash generated by business operations.

This metric focuses on the cash settlement part of a transaction. Not included in *operating cash flow* are cash items related to capital investments, investors, or lenders. In general, *operating cash flow* should

exceed *net profit*; however, *net profit* should ultimately be the largest component of *operating cash flow*. One exception would be in businesses in a continuous pattern of high growth where cash is needed to fund working capital, primarily accounts receivable and inventory.

The inherent limitations of *operating cash flow* include:

- Since it focuses on the settlement part of a business transaction, it can be manipulated by varied accounting practices and management decisions (such as paying vendors late, holding customer checks for deposit at a later date, etc.).

- It can be manipulated and increased at the expense of profit, as in the practice of factoring receivables (selling receivables up front for a discount).

Profit Per Employee

Profit per employee measures the returns on talent in addition to capital. In today's knowledge-based economy, measuring the financial performance of intangibles is more important than ever. Intangibles might include process knowledge, brands, customer bases, or any other form of intellectual capital (such as specialized knowledge and relationships). Large profits can be produced by creating intangibles, as we see in the proliferation of technology, service, and web-based businesses. These businesses require little investment in traditional capital, but large amounts of investment in people talent. *Profit per employee* provides a metric indicating a company's success in converting its raw talent into profits. It is calculated by dividing the *net profit* by the number of full-time equivalent employees engaged in the business operations.

The inherent limitations of *profit per employee*, similar to those of its numerator, *net profit*, include:

- It does not reveal the real cash situation.

- It is an abstract measure because it comes from the income statement and focuses on the promise and agreement part of a business transaction.

- It can be manipulated through management decisions to use part-time or contract staff in place of full-time employees. Determining the number of full-time equivalent employees is an exercise in estimation.

So that's a brief overview of the four bottom lines. Are you tracking <u>all four</u> bottom lines in your business today?

Effective financial management should take all four bottom lines into account. Start with a monthly scorecard that puts all four in view. A sample Financial Scorecard is shown below.

Financial ScoreCard
The Four Bottom Lines for XYZ Company

Summary Income Statement	Current Month		Year-To-Date		Prior Year	
Revenue	$1,650,000	100.00%	$15,450,000	100.00%	$18,375,000	100.00%
Cost of Goods Sold	$1,230,000	74.55%	$11,540,000	74.69%	$14,025,000	76.33%
Gross Margin	$420,000	25.45%	$3,910,000	25.31%	$4,350,000	23.67%
Operating Expenses	$275,000	16.67%	$2,650,000	17.15%	$3,000,000	16.33%
Operating Profit (Loss)	$145,000	8.79%	$1,260,000	8.16%	$1,350,000	7.35%
Net Profit (Loss)	**$140,000**	**8.48%**	**$1,185,000**	**7.67%**	**$1,385,000**	**7.54%**

Operating Cash Flow	Current Month	Year-To-Date	Prior Year
Net Profit (Loss)	$140,000	$1,185,000	$1,385,000
Non-Cash Items			
Depreciation and Amortization	$15,000	$130,000	$145,000
(Gain) or Loss on Sale of Assets			($5,000)
Current Balance Sheet Adjustments			
Accounts Receivable	$35,000	($250,000)	($350,000)
Prepaid Expenses and Deposits	($5,000)	($15,000)	($10,000)
Accounts Payable	($25,000)	$35,000	($115,000)
Other Current Liabilities (non-debt)	($10,000)	$25,000	($25,000)
Operating Cash Flow	**$150,000**	**$1,110,000**	**$1,325,000**

Return on Invested Capital	Current Month	Year-To-Date	Prior Year
Return on Invested Capital	15.57%	17.13%	14.59%

Profit Per Employee	Current Month	Year-To-Date	Prior Year
Profit Per Employee (FTE*)	$933	$7,900	$9,893

* FTE = Full Time Equivalent

Cash Hygiene Items for Entrepreneurs

1. Sign checks. Yes, you should consider signing all outgoing checks if you don't currently do so. Ask for and review the supporting documentation for the checks to be brought to you. This is not as complicated administratively as it sounds. In fact, if you establish a weekly or biweekly payables cycle, you will also save time in the accounting area. You can easily sign the checks, review any detail you would like, and ask any follow-up questions in a relatively short amount of time. And for cash controls, it may be some of your best time spent.

2. Limit checking accounts and signatories. This is a simple cash control mechanism that increases the difficulty of inappropriate behaviors on the financial side of the business.

3. Open the bank statement yourself and review activity *before* it goes to your accounting staff for reconciliation. These first three items definitely benefit your understanding of how cash is flowing through your organization. More importantly, these are a few of the basic steps entrepreneurs should take to prevent fraud.

4. Instill the discipline of preparing and reviewing a weekly cash flow forecast with a 3-4 week rolling view. Your internal accounting staff should be more than capable of handling this. If you would like help setting it up, please feel free to contact me.

5. Develop your understanding of operating cash flow, including profitability and changes in working capital from the balance sheet. You should naturally think "cash going out" when receivables or inventory increase or payables decrease, and "cash coming in" when receivables or inventory decrease or payables increase.

6. Begin a weekly status review of accounts receivable with your internal accounting staff.

7. With the knowledge you gain from item number six, begin educating your customers on your accounts receivable terms. Establish communication with the customer right from the beginning that lets them know you watch cash flow carefully.

We Can Help You Improve Your Financial Visibility and Control!

Even if you have a strong grasp on the material in this course, it's a huge job to effectively manage the cash flow of your business. That's where ActionCFO can help. ActionCFO is a system that couples a seasoned CFO advisor with a proven process for increasing financial visibility and control in your business. In short, it provides the financial management tools and CFO expertise you need in one package for less than 40% of what a full-time CFO would cost. You can learn more about it at **ActionCFO.com.**

The next page shows some additional resources that you may find helpful, including those referenced in this course. Finally, please feel free to contact me directly if you have any further questions or are looking for additional help. My email address is ***troy.schrock@actioncfo.com.***

Additional Resources

Before You Hire a CFO
by Troy D. Schrock

Cash Rules
by Bill McGuinness

Financial Intelligence for Entrepreneurs
by Karen Berman & Joe Knight

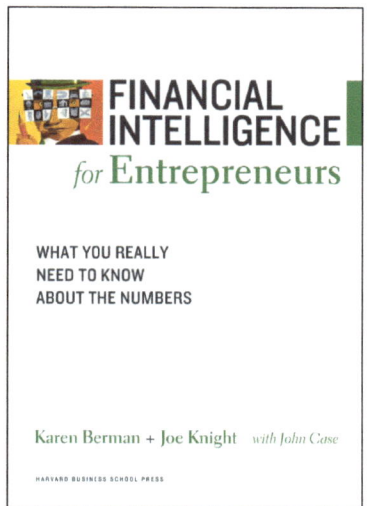

Managing By the Numbers
by Chuck Kremer and Ron Rizzuto with John Case

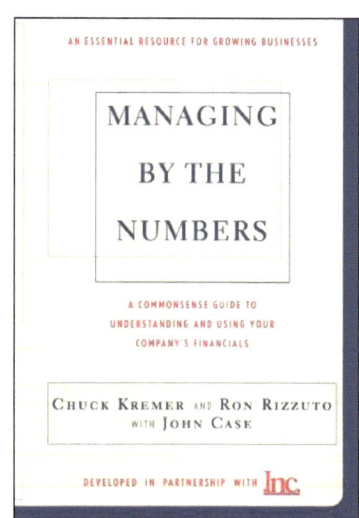

www.actioncfo.com

www.ingramcontent.com/pod-product-compliance
Lightning Source LLC
Chambersburg PA
CBHW050830180526
45159CB00004B/1851